MADAM&EVE

Somewhere over the Rainbow Nation

BY S. FRANCIS, H. DUGMORE & RICO

"CARTOONISTS OF THE YEAR"
"Is nothing sacred? Not where Madam & Eve are concerned anyway.
A great collection to give and to keep."
THE STAR

"LAUGH AND BE RECONCILED"
"Apartheid's antidote … South Africans worship Madam & Eve as a
matter of patriotic pride."
STUDENT LIFE

"WORLD CLASS"
"… the characterisation, the drawing and the unerring perception
that make them so true, so funny and so beloved."
THE EASTERN PROVINCE HERALD

"CARTOON OF THE YEAR"
"Outrageously funny … with unerring humour and intelligence.
If you haven't already fallen in love with Madam & Eve, this is
a fine opportunity."
COSMOPOLITAN

"THE MOST POPULAR CARTOON IN SOUTH AFRICA"
"Humour, repressed for years, makes a giddy comeback."
THE WALL STREET JOURNAL

"AT LAST IT'S TIME FOR A LAUGH"
"People of all colours and political stripe can't get
enough of Madam & Eve."
NEWSWEEK MAGAZINE

"DELICIOUSLY IRONIC"
"More than a book to enjoy – it's a collector's item …
Madam & Eve's creators clearly have their fingers spot on
the pulse of South African life."
THE CITIZEN

"EXTRAORDINARY … A SOUTH AFRICAN PHENOMENON"
"Scores high on the hilarity barometer with
liberal doses of political realism."
THE MAIL & GUARDIAN

"DOWNRIGHT HILARIOUS"
"A great book to send to South Africans overseas or to those who
want to look through the window at our complex lives."
THE CAPE TIMES

"LARGER THAN LIFE"
"Madam & Eve have insinuated their way into the hearts and minds
of the nation … if you give no other gift this Christmas,
give Madam & Eve."
THE SUNDAY TIMES

"LOCATES THE COMMON NATIONAL FUNNY BONE"
"Pokes fun across lines of colour and caste … widely published
and widely quoted."
THE WASHINGTON POST

PENGUIN BOOKS

Published by the Penguin Group
27 Wrights Lane, London W8 5TZ, England
Viking Penguin, a division of Penguin Books USA Inc,
375 Hudson Street, New York, New York 10014, USA
Penguin Books Australia Ltd, Ringwood, Victoria, Australia
Penguin Books Canada Ltd, 10 Alcorn Avenue, Toronto, Ontario, Canada M4V 3B2
Penguin Books (NZ) Ltd, 182-190 Wairau Road, Auckland 10, New Zealand
Penguin Books South Africa (Pty) Ltd, Pallinghurst Road, Parktown, South Africa 2193

Penguin Books South Africa (Pty) Ltd,
Registered Offices: 20 Woodlands Drive, Woodmead, Sandton 2128

First published by Penguin Books 1996

Copyright © S Francis, H Dugmore & R Schacherl 1996

ISBN 0 140 26420 5

Typesetting and reproduction by Positive Proof cc
Printed and bound by Interpak, Natal

Other Madam & Eve Books

The Madam & Eve Collection
Free At Last
All aboard for the Gravy Train
Jamen sort kaffe er på mode nu, Madam! (Glydendal Publishing, Denmark)

Madam & Eve appears regularly in:

The Mail & Guardian, The Star, The Saturday Star, The Eastern Province Herald, The Natal Mercury, The Natal Witness, The Cape Times, The Daily Dispatch, The Diamond Fields Advertiser, The S.A. Times, Fair Lady, Vodaworld and Student Life Magazines.

To Contact Madam & Eve:

- *PO Box 94, WITS Post Office, 2050, South Africa*
- *email: hardug@aztec.co.za*
- *visit Madam & Eve at the Mail & Guardian Web page: http:/www.mg.co.za/mg*

You are now travelling on the South African information **highway**.

Stick 'em up. This is a **hijack**.

That's right. Nobody move. This is a **hijack**.

I TOLD YOU NOT TO TRAVEL ON THE INFORMATION HIGHWAY!

HOW WAS I SUPPOSED TO KNOW IT'S DANGEROUS?!

THIS IS SOUTH AFRICA! ALL HIGHWAYS ARE DANGEROUS!

NOW YOU TELL ME!

HEY! We said **NO TALKING!!**

SEE? NOW YOU'RE MAKING THEM NERVOUS!

WHAT'S GOING ON, MADAM?

SHHH! WE'RE BEING HIJACKED ON THE INFORMATION HIGHWAY!

That's right! We're **desperate** criminals!

WHAT CAN THEY DO TO YOU? JUST **TURN OFF** THE COMPUTER.

Damn. They found our one **weakness**.

NYAH! NYAH! NYAH!

I'M CALLING THE POLICE.

MADAM & Eve

BY S.FRANCIS, H.DUGMORE & RICO

EVE!!

THIS IS WEIRD, MARGE. I CAN'T FIND MY RED BELT... AND I'VE LOOKED EVERY-WHERE.

WHY DON'T YOU DO WHAT I DO...

I ASK MY MAID IF SHE'S "SEEN" IT. AND SHE ALWAYS SAYS "NO MADAM."

THEN THE NEXT DAY I LOOK -- AND IT'S BACK IN MY CUPBOARD.

TRUST ME. IT NEVER FAILS.

EVE! I'VE LOOKED EVERYWHERE! HAVE YOU SEEN MY RED BELT?!

NO MADAM.

BUT IF I SEE IT, I'LL PUT IT BACK IN MARGE'S CUPBOARD.

15

...AND IN OTHER NEWS, A **COUP D'ETAT** TOOK PLACE ON THE COMORES THIS WEEK...

ACCORDING TO REPORTS, FRENCH **MERCENARY** SOLDIERS ARE IN CONTROL OF THE ISLAND AND HAVE SURROUNDED THE AIRPORT, HOTELS AND BEACHES.

THE **COMORES**? ISN'T THAT WHERE MADAM JUST WENT ON HOLIDAY?

UH-OH.

LADIES AND GENTLEMEN-- WELCOME TO SHOWNIGHT AT THE HOTEL COMORES. I'LL BE TAKING SONG REQUESTS IN JUST A MOMENT, BUT FIRST...

HI. WHO ARE YOU AND WHAT DO YOU DO?

I'M PIERRE, A **FRENCH MERCENARY** AND I'M HERE WITH MY FRIENDS.

ARE YOU HERE ON HOLIDAY, PIERRE?

NO. A **COUP D'ETAT**. WE JUST TOOK OVER THE ISLAND.

WELL, BEST OF LUCK TO YOU, PIERRE!

PLAY SOMETHING BY CHARLES AZNAVOUR OR I'LL KILL YOU.

HAVE YOU HEARD FROM MADAM IN THE **COMORES** YET, MOTHER ANDERSON?

NOT YET...

I WOULDN'T **WORRY**, MOTHER ANDERSON. I'M SURE SHE'S NOT IN ANY DANGER.

NOT IN ANY DANGER?!!

WHY, AT THIS VERY MOMENT SHE'S TRAPPED IN HER HOTEL, SURROUNDED BY A BUNCH OF BATTLE-HARDENED FRENCH MERCENARIES!!

WHO GETS THE ESCARGOT IN GARLIC SAUCE?

OVER HERE!

MADAM & EVE

BY S. FRANCIS, H. DUGMORE & RICO

LADIES & GENTLEMEN! IT'S AUTOMATIC TELLER TIME!!

HI! I'M BOB, YOUR NEW HOST... AND I'D LIKE TO WELCOME YOU TO YOUR NEIGHBOURHOOD ATM!!

WE'LL BE INSERTING THE CARD IN JUST A MOMENT...BUT FIRST, LET'S FIND OUT A LITTLE **MORE** ABOUT OUR TWO CONTESTANTS.

HI. WHAT'S YOUR NAME? — UH... GWEN ANDERSON.

AND YOU? — ...EVE SISULU.

YOU TWO ARE **SISTERS**, RIGHT?

HEY-- ONLY JOKING! YOU'RE GREAT SPORTS! AND WHAT'S YOUR **PIN NUMBER**?

NICE TRY. I'M CALLING THE **POLICE**.

AND WE'LL BE RIGHT BACK AFTER THIS COMMERCIAL BREAK.

THESE ATM **THIEVES** ARE GETTING REALLY **INVENTIVE**.

MADAM & EVE

BY S. FRANCIS, H. DUGMORE & RICO

WHEN I GROW UP, I'M GOING TO MAKE LOTS OF MONEY.

OH-- A DOCTOR? ...A LAWYER?

A GOVERNMENT CONSULTANT.

DO YOU EVEN KNOW WHAT A CONSULTANT DOES?

OF COURSE! FIRST, THEY CONSULT...

...AND THEN THEY SEND THE **BILL.**

SOMETIMES THEY EVEN ADD AN **EXTRA** NOUGHT BY MISTAKE.

IT'S A **GREAT CAREER!** I'M TELLING YOU THIS CONSULTING IS THE WAVE OF THE FUTURE!

I'D LIKE TO GET STARTED EARLY. NEED ANY CONSULTING WORK DONE?

NO.

I BET IF I WAS A GIN & TONIC CONSULTANT, YOU'D HIRE ME.

ARE YOU **SURE** THERE'S NOTHING I CAN ADVISE YOU ON?

YES THERE IS! YOU CAN TELL ME HOW I CAN GET SOME **PEACE** AND **QUIET** AROUND HERE!!

THIS CALLS FOR A SUB-COMMITTEE. I'LL NEED AN ADVANCE.

© Rapid Phase Entertainment - 1995

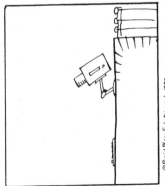

MADAM & Eve

BY S.FRANCIS, H.DUGMORE & RICO

FREEZE!! THIS IS A HIJACK!!

...WHAT ARE YOU HIJACKING? THIS CARTOON.

ARE YOU CRAZY?! NOBODY HIJACKS A CARTOON!!

WHY NOT? PEOPLE STEAL COPPER WIRE, TELEPHONE LINES AND SIGN POSTS... I BET THIS IS WORTH SOMETHING!

AND IF IT ISN'T, WE'LL JUST TAKE IT TO A CHOP SHOP AND SELL OFF THE CARTOON PANELS.

© Rapid Phase Entertainment - 1996

I CAN'T BELIEVE THIS! IS THERE NO END TO CRIME IN THIS COUNTRY?!!

OKAY, PULL!

RRRIP!!

THIS IS TRAUMATIC. I COULD USE SOME TEA.

SORRY. THEY TOOK THE KITCHEN.

I CAN'T BELIEVE IT! I CALL NELSON MANDELA TO TELL HIM MY BICYCLE WAS HIJACKED... AND THEY TELL ME HE'S UNAVAILABLE!

GIVE ME THE PHONE.

HELLO? IS THE PRESIDENT AVAILABLE? I'M WINNIE MANDELA'S ATTORNEY AND I THINK WE'VE REACHED A FAIR SETTLEMENT.

HOLD ON! I'LL GET HIM!!

ALL YOURS.

HELLO? THIS IS NELSON.

DEAR NELSON MANDELA. MY NEW BICYCLE WAS HIJACKED YESTERDAY.

I AM ENCLOSING AN IDENTIKIT OF THE PERPETRATORS THAT I DREW MYSELF.

WHAT DO YOU THINK?

THAT SHOULD BE ENOUGH TO GET THEM STARTED.

MAYBE THEY'LL BRING IN AN OVERSEAS EXPERT!

MADAM & EVE

BY S. FRANCIS, H. DUGMORE & RICO

ROBBEN ISLAND, 1962... A NEW PRISONER ARRIVES...

HELLO, BAFANA.

WHO?

WAS THIS THE DANGEROUS TERRORIST I'D HEARD SO MUCH ABOUT? AFTER ALL, HE WAS JUST A MAN...

OKAY EVERYONE! STRIP SEARCH!!

SORRY, BAFANA.

WHO?

I SENSED HE WAS DESTINED FOR **GREATNESS**. I RESOLVED TO **HELP** HIM AS MUCH AS I COULD...

MY TURN. GIVE ME THE SLEDGEHAMMER.

I EVEN BEGAN TO QUESTION MY VALUES. COULD IT BE THAT THE SYSTEM WAS WRONG?!!

STRIP SEARCH!

GEEZ. I REALLY HATE TO DO THIS.

AS THE YEARS WENT BY I REALISED I KNEW HIM BETTER THAN ANYONE.

BAFANA-- ONE DAY, I PREDICT YOU'LL TAKE THE LONG WALK TO FREEDOM.

"LONG WALK TO FREEDOM"?...I LIKE THAT!

AT HIS PRESIDENTIAL INAUGURATION, I WAS SITTING RIGHT UP FRONT!

I CENSORED HIS LETTERS FOR THIRTY YEARS!

I JUST HAD TO TELL THE WORLD MY STORY. IT WAS MY **SACRED** DUTY TO WRITE A BOOK.

OKAY. MY CLIENT'S HAPPY WITH THE ROYALTY. LET'S TALK **ADVANCE**.

AT THE LAUNCH PARTY FOR MY BOOK, HE DIDN'T ARRIVE. I WAS DEVASTATED.

WAIT! COME BACK! I'M SURE HE'LL BE HERE ANY MINUTE!

IT WAS THEN I REALISED THAT PEOPLE IN HIS INNER CIRCLE CONSPIRED TO DESTROY OUR FRIENDSHIP.

THOSE LETTERS YOU PUBLISHED? WE'RE SUING...

IT'S ALRIGHT BAFANA! I KNOW IT'S NOT YOU!

SO YES, I'LL NEVER FORGET BAFANA. MY PRISONER... MY FRIEND... AND SOON TO BE A MAJOR MOTION PICTURE!!

Gene Hackman   Wesley Snipes

GOODBYE BAFANA

The Long Walk to Friendship

EVE--THIS IS MOM'S TWIN SISTER VISITING FROM ENGLAND. SHE'LL BE STAYING WITH US A WHILE.

TWO OF THEM?! THERE'S TWO OF THEM NOW?!

BY THE WAY... THESE PEARLS ARE WORTHLESS. THEY'RE JUST COSTUME JEWELLERY.

EVE!! WHERE'RE YOU GOING?!

EMERGENCY LEAVE.

Mother Anderson's twin sister arrived from England today for a long visit.

EVE! IT'S FIVE O'CLOCK!

...WHERE'S OUR GIN & TONIC?!

By the time you read this, I will be dead.

ABIGAIL, YOUR TV DOESN'T WORK.

CLICK!
CLICK!
CLICK!
CLICK!
CLICK!

DON'T WORRY... I OFTEN MAKE THE SAME MISTAKE. THAT'S NOT THE TV REMOTE CONTROL. THAT'S THE GARAGE OPENER.

CLICK!

NO HARM DONE.

MADAM!!

37

41

FINALLY.

I JUST CAN'T GET THROUGH THE DAY WITHOUT THE MORNING NEWSPAPER.

SMACK!!

SQUISH!!

EVE! THERE'S A FLY IN MY SUIT!

LOOK, SPARKY. THOSE PEOPLE JUST PUT PLASTIC BOTTLES FILLED WITH WATER ON THEIR LAWN.

THEY'RE WATCHING US. LET'S HUMOUR THEM.

GASP! PLASTIC BOTTLES!!

SNIFF! SNIFF!

LET'S GET OUT OF HERE!!

YOWL!! YOWL!!

SEE, EVE? I TOLD YOU IT KEEPS DOGS AWAY.

43

MADAM & Eve

BY S.FRANCIS, H.DUGMORE & RICO

"AND WE'LL BE BACK WITH **MORE** OF THE PRINCESS DI INTERVIEW AFTER THIS..."

"AND WE THOUGHT WE HAD PROBLEMS..."

"MOTHER ANDERSON, DO YOU KNOW WHO PRINCESS DI IS?"

"YES. SHE'S THE PRINCESS OF WALES."

"YOU MEAN LIKE IN "FREE WILLY"?"

"NOT **WHALES**. ...**WALES**. IT'S A PLACE IN BRITAIN."

"SOMEONE TOLD ME SHE HAS **BLUE BLOOD**."

"IT RUNS IN THE FAMILY."

"ALSO, SHE HAD **BULIMIA**. YOU KNOW WHAT THAT IS?"

"YES."

"EVERY TIME SHE HAS A MEAL, SHE THROWS UP--"

"I SAID I **KNOW** WHAT IT IS!"

"SHE ALSO HAD A SECRET AFFAIR."

"I HOPE SHE DIDN'T MEET THE GUY AT DINNER."

"**GWEN!!**"

44

CHILL OUT
IN THE NEW
SOUTH
AFRICA
Only 10 Rand

DON'T YOU EVER GET
TIRED OF TRYING TO
EXTORT MONEY FROM
PEOPLE WITH THESE
SILLY BUSINESS
IDEAS?!
CHILL OUT
IN THE N
SOUTH

I MEAN, IF I GIVE
YOU TEN RAND, HOW
CAN YOU POSSIBLY
GET ME TO
CHILL OUT?!
CHILL OUT
IN THE N
SOUTH

OKAY.
TURN ON
THE HOSE
PIPE.
CHILL OUT
IN THE NEW
SOUTH
AFRICA

A FOOL AND
HIS MONEY
ARE SOON
PARTED
Only 10 Rand

YOU'VE GOT
TO BE
KIDDING.
A FOOL AND
HIS MONEY
ARE SOON
PARTED
Only 10 Rand

A FOO
HIS MON
ARE SO
PARTE
Only 10 R

WELL, SO
MUCH FOR
"TRUTH IN
ADVERTISING".
A FOOL AND
HIS MONEY
ARE SOON
PARTED
Only 10 Rand

MAKE YOUR
VOICE HEARD
IN THE NEW
SOUTH
AFRICA
Only 10 Rand

SO HOW
DO I MAKE
MY VOICE
HEARD?
WHAT?
MAKE YOU
VOICE HEA
IN THE NE
SOUTH
AFRICA

I SAID --
HOW DO I
MAKE MY
VOICE
HEARD?!
WHAT?
MAKE YO
VOICE HEA
IN THE NE
SOUTH

HOW DO I
MAKE MY
VOICE
HEARD?!!
YOU JUST
DID.
THAT'LL
BE
TEN RAND.
MAKE YO
VOICE HE
IN THE N

47

MADAM & Eve

BY S. FRANCIS, H. DUGMORE & RICO

AHA!

WHAT'S THAT, MADAM?

I'VE BEEN DOING A LITTLE ESOTERIC RESEARCH ON YOUR OLD CV.

UH-OH.

ACCORDING TO YOUR CV, YOU PREVIOUSLY WORKED FOR THE OPPENHEIMERS.

THAT'S RIGHT.

YOU WORKED FOR HARRY OPPENHEIMER OF HOUGHTON?

NOT EXACTLY...

...BOB OPPENHEIMER OF ALBERTON.

AND WHAT ABOUT THIS... IT SAYS HERE YOU HAVE A PHD!!

IT'S TRUE! I DO HAVE A PHD!

A... PROFESSIONAL HOUSEKEEPING DIPLOMA.

OH-- AND I SUPPOSE I SHOULD BELIEVE THIS ONE! IT SAYS YOU HAVE... "PREVIOUS CABINET EXPERIENCE..."

I DO. I USED TO POLISH THEM EVERY DAY.

ADMIT IT, EVE! YOU DELIBERATELY EXAGGERATED YOUR CV IN ORDER TO GET THIS JOB!

THIS ISN'T FAIR. YOU'RE JUST PICKING ON ME BECAUSE I'M BLACK.

BLACK?! ...IT SAYS HERE YOU'RE A "WHITE NANNY FROM ENGLAND!!"

HEY-- ONE SMALL MISPRINT. SO SUE ME.

48

50

EVE'S DRIVING ME **CRAZY** WITH THOSE STUPID **PUPPETS!** ESPECIALLY THE ONE THAT LOOKS LIKE ME!

OH, LEAVE HER ALONE.

WHERE'S YOUR SENSE OF HUMOUR? LET HER HAVE A LITTLE FUN-- DON'T BE SO SENSITIVE!

LET HER HAVE A LITTLE FUN-- DON'T BE SO SENSITIVE.

THAT'S NOT FUNNY!! THAT'S NOT FUNNY.

EVE-- IF YOU DON'T STOP PLAYING WITH THOSE PUPPETS, I'M CALLING A PSYCHIATRIST.

I'M **ALREADY** SEEING A PSYCHIATRIST! AND HE SAYS PUPPETS ARE A HEALTHY WAY TO RELEASE MY FRUSTRATIONS.

IMPOSSIBLE.

IF YOU DON'T BELIEVE ME, ASK HIM YOURSELF!

GO AHEAD. TELL HER.

DOES SHE HAVE AN APPOINTMENT?

OKAY. A LITTLE TO THE LEFT.

NOW TRY TO THE RIGHT.

THAT'S IT! PERFECT!

OKAY, YOU CAN COME DOWN NOW.

HELLO? THIS IS... ER, POLICE SERGEANT VAN STADEN. I NEED AN IMMEDIATE CHECK ON A RED TOYOTA, NUMBER PLATE SGT 570T.

...AND I ESPECIALLY NEED A CELLPHONE NUMBER ON THAT. ...THANK YOU.

HEY! YOU IN THE RED TOYOTA! YEAH, YOU!! WHERE'D YOU LEARN TO DRIVE?!!

EVE!! I'M IN THE BASE-MENT!!

CLICK!!

IT'S NOT ENOUGH SHE'S OLD AND CRANKY... SHE ALSO HAS TO BE SHORT.

MADAM & EVE

BY S. FRANCIS, H. DUGMORE & RICO

AND SO, MARY AND JOSEPH HAD TO SLEEP IN THE STABLE. DO YOU KNOW WHY?

OF COURSE!

THERE WAS NO ROOM AT THE **HOLIDAY INN**.

IT'S JUST AS WELL. THEY PROBABLY WOULDN'T LET THE **DONKEY** IN ANYWAY.

CAN I PLEASE CONTINUE?

GO ON. THEN THE THREE WISE GUYS CAME.

WISE **MEN**.

HOW COME THERE WEREN'T ANY WISE **WOMEN**?

GOOD QUESTION.

ANYWAY, EACH OF THE THREE WISE MEN BROUGHT SOMETHING. GOLD...

AND THEY BROUGHT **FRANKENSTEIN**!

FRANKINCENSE.

...AND **MURRAY**!

WHO WAS MURRAY? WAS HE LIKE, A FRIEND OF THEIRS?

FORGET MURRAY! THEY DIDN'T BRING MURRAY! THEY BROUGHT **MYRRH**!!

MYRRH? **MOM!** YOU PROMISED YOU WOULDN'T GET UPSET THIS CHRISTMAS!

OKAY, SO WHO WAS MYRRH?

MURRAY'S WIFE.

ACCORDING TO HIS CV, THIS IS THE *REAL* FATHER CHRISTMAS.

NOT SO FAST. HOW DO WE KNOW HIS CV ISN'T EXAGGERATED?

BEFORE I ANSWER THAT I'LL NEED TO CONSULT WITH MY *ATTORNEY.*

EVERY YEAR, IT GETS HARDER TO BELIEVE IN PEOPLE.

IF YOU ASK ME, FATHER CHRISTMAS HAS IT MADE!

A CUSHY JOB... A LARGE STAFF OF ELVES... HE TRAVELS AROUND THE WORLD...

AND HE ONLY WORKS *ONE DAY* A YEAR!

DON'T SAY IT.

HE'S ON THE *GRAVY SLEIGH!*

GOBBLE... GOBBLE...
...GOBBLE...
GOBBLE...

...GOBBLE...
AWK!!
SQUAWK!

TURKEY'S ALMOST
READY, MADAM.

LUNCH IS SERVED.
TWO BIG **TURKEY**
SANDWICHES.

AGAIN?!!

LEFTOVER **TURKEY**
FOR BREAKFAST!
TURKEY FOR LUNCH!
TURKEY FOR DINNER!
IT'S DRIVING ME
CRAZY!!

IF I SEE
ANOTHER PIECE
OF **TURKEY**
THIS HOLIDAY,
I'LL **SCREAM**!!

CALM DOWN, MOM.
YOU'RE OVER-REACTING.

WHAT'S A NEW YEAR'S RESOLUTION?

RAISE YOUR RIGHT HAND AND REPEAT AFTER ME: I PROMISE TO STOP ASKING SO MANY QUESTIONS AND BOTHERING PEOPLE.

...I PROMISE TO STOP ASKING SO MANY QUESTIONS AND BOTHERING PEOPLE.

CONGRATULATIONS. YOU JUST MADE A NEW YEAR'S RESOLUTION.

WAIT A MINUTE! I JUST ASKED WHAT IT IS!

SORRY. IT'S BINDING.

NUMBER ONE: I PROMISE TO BEHAVE BETTER.

NUMBER TWO: I PROMISE TO STOP BEING SO GRUMPY AND BAD-TEMPERED.

NUMBER THREE: I PROMISE TO DRINK ONLY ONE GIN & TONIC A DAY.

IF IT'S ALRIGHT WITH YOU, I'LL DO MY OWN NEW YEAR'S RESOLUTIONS!!

MIELLLIES!

FWEEP!!

HAPPY NEW YEAR!!

MIELLLIES!!

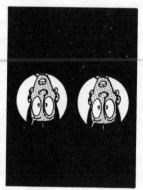

NOT NOW, MOM. I'VE ALMOST GOT HER!

THEIR WAGE NEGOTIATIONS GET CRAZIER EVERY YEAR.

THIS WON'T TAKE LONG, MOM. I JUST HAVE TO ASSEMBLE MY NEW ANTI-CAR-THEFT DEVICE.

CLICK CLACK CLACK CLICK CLICK CLICK

THIS CAN'T BE RIGHT.

WHERE ARE THE INSTRUCTIONS?

I'M SITTING ON THEM.

MADAM & EVE

BY S. FRANCIS, H. DUGMORE & RICO

AND IN OTHER NEWS, THE NATIONAL PARTY ANNOUNCED TODAY THAT IT INTENDS TO RE-INVENT ITSELF WITH A TOTAL IMAGE MAKE-OVER.

WHY WOULD THEY DO THAT?

NECESSITY IS THE MOTHER OF RE-INVENTION.

DING DONG!

I'VE GOT IT.

HELLO LADIES -- IF I COULD JUST HAVE A MOMENT OF YOUR TIME--

...TO TALK TO YOU ABOUT AN ORGANISATION THAT'S BEEN AN INSTITUTION IN THIS COUNTRY FOR DECADES!

WE'RE UNDERGOING A TOTAL IMAGE MAKE-OVER! WE'RE RE-INVENTING OURSELVES!

AND WE NEED YOUR SUPPORT!

WE'RE EVEN THINKING OF CHANGING OUR NAME TO A SYMBOL?

HEY! IT WORKED FOR PRINCE, DIDN'T IT?

IT'S THE NEW SOUTH AFRICA! ADAPT OR DIE, I ALWAYS SAY.

YOU'RE FROM THE NATIONAL PARTY, AREN'T YOU?

UH, NO. WITS UNIVERSITY.

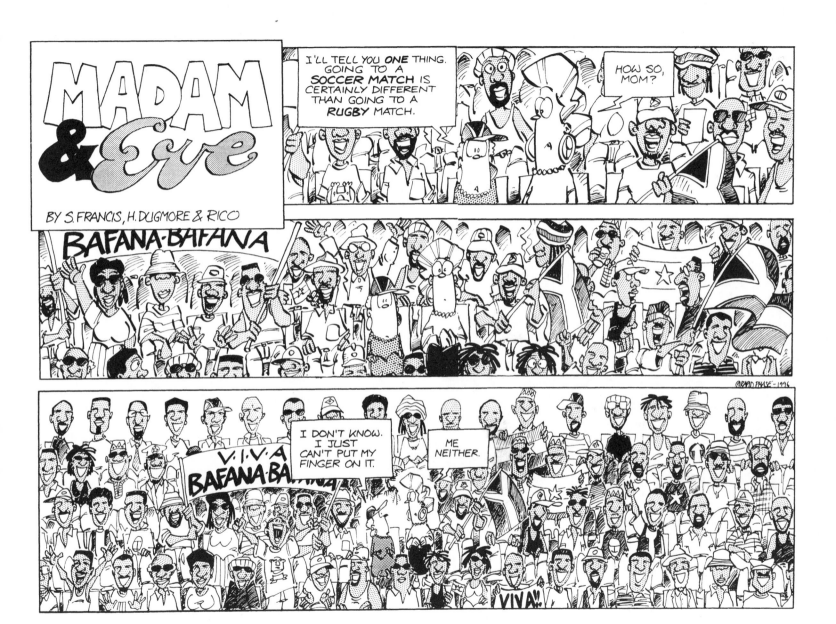

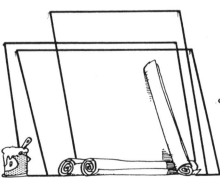

THE SECRET NATIONAL PARTY MAKE-OVER CONTINUES...

AND, TO TOTALLY RE-INVENT OURSELVES, WE'VE EMPLOYED A TOP ADVERTISING AGENCY TO ADVISE US... REGGIE?

THANK YOU. WE FELT THE FIRST THING NEEDED IS A *BOLD NEW NAME*. ... AND WE'VE COME UP WITH A WINNER. THE "NATIONAL PARTY" WILL NOW BE CALLED...

THE *AMAZING NATIONAL CAUCUS!*

THE AMAZING NATIONAL CAUCUS

THE A...N...C...?

EXACTLY! ANYTHING THEY DO, *YOU'LL* GET THE CREDIT.

A TOP AD AGENCY ADVISES THE NATIONAL PARTY...

RIGHT. LET'S TALK IMAGE, SLOGAN AND LOGO.

OUR BRIEF WAS TO CREATE A GRAPHIC DESIGN THAT WAS BOTH VOTER-FRIENDLY AND INSTANTLY RECOGNISABLE! ...MAY I PRESENT YOUR NEW LOGO!!...

THE NATIONAL SMILEY FACE PARTY.

HEY! THAT LOOKS LIKE *YOU*, MR. DE KLERK.

OH SHUT UP.

MADAM & Eve

BY S. FRANCIS, H. DUGMORE & RICO

<SO TELL ME-- HOW'S WORK?!> <BUSY, BUSY BUSY! HOW ABOUT YOU?!>

...ELEVEN OFFICIAL LANGUAGES. AND THEY'RE ALL LOUD.

EVE--EXPLAIN SOMETHING TO ME. WHY DO YOU AND YOUR FRIENDS ALWAYS TALK SO LOUD?

WHAT DO YOU MEAN?

YOU'RE STANDING RIGHT NEXT TO EACH OTHER. DO YOU HAVE TO SHOUT SO THE WHOLE NEIGHBOURHOOD CAN HEAR?

I MEAN-- WHAT IF MOM AND I TALKED LIKE THAT?

HI MOM! I'M HOW FINE! ARE HOW ARE YOU?! YOU?!

WHAT DO YOU WANT TO DO TODAY?! I KNOW! LET'S WATCH TV!!

...SEE? YOU DON'T UNDERSTAND, MADAM. IT'S A CULTURAL THING.

WE AFRICANS HAVE A LONG HISTORY OF ORAL TRADITION! WE EXPRESS OURSELVES WITH VIM, VIGOUR AND ZEST!

OUR PEOPLE TALK LOUDLY BECAUSE WE'RE BOLD... ANIMATED... AND FULL OF LIFE!

I ALWAYS THOUGHT WE DID IT TO ANNOY WHITE PEOPLE.

SHH. NOT SO LOUD.

72

MADAM & EVE

BY S.FRANCIS, H.DUGMORE & RICO

MY AFRICAN CUP RUNNETH OVER.

TO JOHN MOSHOEU.

TO DOCTOR KHUMALO.

TO PHIL MASINGA.

WHAT'S GOING ON? WE'RE CELEBRATING BAFANA BAFANA'S VICTORY WITH A LITTLE BET.

I BET YOUR MOTHER THAT SHE CAN'T PRONOUNCE ALL THE PLAYER'S NAMES PROPERLY...WHOEVER LOSES THE BET, HAS TO DOWN A TRIPLE GIN & TONIC.

HOW'S SHE DOING? SURPRISINGLY WELL. SHE'S ALMOST FINISHED. TO AUGUSTINE MAKALAKALANE!

TO MARK FISCHT.

OOPS.

NOW HOLD ON JUST A DARN MINUTE!!

AND IN OTHER NEWS... MORE AND MORE SOUTH AFRICAN CITIZENS HAVE DISCOVERED **BUGGING** DEVICES HIDDEN IN THEIR HOMES.

IF ANYONE'S LISTENING IN... COULD SOMEONE GET ME ANOTHER GIN & TONIC?!

...AND WE'LL BE RIGHT BACK WITH MORE ON THE WIDESPREAD **BUGGING** OF SOUTH AFRICAN CITIZENS.

DIDN'T YOU HEAR ME?!

I SAID... WHOEVER'S BUGGING THIS HOUSE... COULD YOU AT LEAST BRING ME ANOTHER GIN & TONIC!

COME BACK HERE YOU IDIOT! SHE'S BLUFFING!

WE'VE SWEPT YOUR WHOLE HOUSE MRS ANDERSON. THERE ARE NO BUGGING DEVICES.

ARE YOU ABSOLUTELY SURE?!   YES.

YOU MEAN... **NO-ONE'S** INTERESTED IN ME... AT ALL?!   SORRY.

SOB!   IF IT HELPS, MADAM. I LISTEN AT THE KEYHOLE SOMETIMES.

Panel 1: MADAM! COME QUICKLY! LOOK WHAT I FOUND IN THE LAMP!

Panel 2: A HIDDEN BUGGING DEVICE. ≡GASP≡ SOMEBODY'S BEEN... SPYING ON ME?

Panel 3: YES! I'VE FINALLY ARRIVED!!

Panel 4: A REFRIGERATOR MAGNET WITH A WIRE STUCK ON IT? BEST I COULD DO.

Panel 5: MARGE-LOOK! SOMEONE'S BEEN BUGGING MY HOUSE! TALK ABOUT A STATUS SYMBOL! LET ME SEE! LET ME SEE!

Panel 6: ...THAT'S ODD. IT LOOKS EXACTLY LIKE A REFRIGERATOR MAGNET.

Panel 7:

Panel 8: PROFESSIONALS. NO DOUBT ABOUT IT.

Panel 9: HI MADAM! CAN I HAVE THAT WAGE INCREASE YOU PROMISED ME?

Panel 10:

Panel 11: WHY OF COURSE YOU CAN, EVE. NO PROBLEM!

Panel 12: EVERYONE'S ALWAYS NICER WHEN THEY THINK THEIR HOUSE IS BUGGED.

EVE!!

HAVE YOU SEEN MY CELLPHONE?

NO MADAM... BUT WHY DON'T YOU RETRACE YOUR STEPS?

GOOD IDEA. LET'S SEE... I PUT IT IN MY JACKET POCKET... THEN I TOOK OFF MY JACKET...

RING. RING.

MIELLLIES!! ...OW!!

"MIELIES ...OW?"

MIELLLIES!! ...OUCH!!

"MIELIES ...OUCH?"

MIELLLIES!! ...EINA!!

HEY! I'M JUST GETTING STARTED!

IF YOU'VE JUST JOINED US, THIS IS RADIO MADAM... WHERE THE HITS JUST KEEP ON COMING. THIS ONE GOES OUT TO EVE SISULU.

BANG! CLANG! BANG! CLANG! CLANG!

...NEXT BEST THING TO A DIGITAL ALARM CLOCK.

MADAM & Eve

BY S. FRANCIS, H. DUGMORE & RICO

IT WAS A HOT, DRY DAY WHEN THE STRANGER CAME TO TOWN...

WHO SHE WAS OR WHERE SHE CAME FROM, NOBODY KNOWS.

SENSING TROUBLE, THE PIANO PLAYER STOPPED WHEN SHE WALKED THROUGH THE DOORS OF THE DOUBLE-R-SALOON.

THE GAMBLERS DROPPED THEIR CARDS...

...AND THE BARTENDER KEPT HIS HANDS IN PLAIN SIGHT.

EVEN THE SALOON GIRLS KEPT THEIR DISTANCE...

FINALLY, A YOUNG COWBOY AT THE BAR HAD THE COURAGE TO ASK HER NAME.

MY NAME IS EVE.

...SHE SAID.

...AND I'M GOING TO CLEAN UP THIS TOWN!

EVE! WAKE UP! GET BACK TO WORK!!

POP!!

HUH?

BUT... I HAVEN'T CLEANED UP THE TOWN YET.

FORGET THE TOWN. JUST CLEAN UP THE KITCHEN.

MADAM & Eve

BY S. FRANCIS, H. DUGMORE & RICO

SEE MOM? THE LATEST IN HI-TECH LASER BEAM SECURITY! NOBODY CAN WALK THROUGH THIS HOUSE WITHOUT SETTING OFF THE ALARM.

'NIGHT, MADAM.

I HATE IT WHEN SHE DOES THAT.

MADAM & Eve

BY S. FRANCIS, H. DUGMORE & RICO

WELCOME TO OUR WOMEN'S SELF-DEFENCE CLASS. ...YOU'LL NEED A PARTNER, SO TURN AND FACE THE WOMAN NEXT TO YOU.

OKAY, GIRLS. FIRST, I'LL DEMONSTRATE SOME BASIC, SELF-DEFENCE MOVES. I'LL NEED A VOLUNTEER.

NOW WATCH CLOSELY. --PRETEND I'M A MUGGER -- AND I COME UP BEHIND YOU LIKE THIS.

SEE? THERE'S NOTHING YOU CAN DO, RIGHT?

HEE-YA!!

HOOOOWEEE!!

BONK!! HAI!!

YOUR MOTHER KNOWS KUNG-FU?

MORE LIKE CANE-FU.

MADAM & Eve

BY S. FRANCIS, H. DUGMORE & RICO

HI! WE'RE RUNNING AN **INCREDIBLY SPECIAL PROMOTION** AND YOU MAY HAVE **ALREADY** WON A NEW CAR, A WIDE-SCREEN COLOUR TV OR DINNER FOR TWO AT AN EXCLUSIVE RESTAURANT. HOW DOES THAT SOUND?!

...HELLO? IS ANYONE THERE?

YOU WANT TO... SPEAK... TO MADAM?

ER... YES. COULD I SPEAK TO MADAM?

MADAM NOT HERE.

NOT TO WORRY! COULD YOU **TELL** HER WHEN SHE RETURNS THAT SHE'S WON **FABULOUS PRIZES** AND TO CALL ME AT THE FOLLOWING NUMBER...

MADAM NOT HERE.

I **KNOW** SHE'S NOT THERE! COULD YOU **GIVE HER A MESSAGE?!**

A MASSAGE?

MESSAGE!! GIVE MADAM A MESSAGE!!

MADAM NOT HERE.

FORGET IT!! JUST FORGET THE WHOLE THING!!

CLICK!

DID YOU ENJOY YOURSELF?

TIME SHARE SALES CALLS ARE THE **HIGHLIGHT** OF MY DAY.

MADAM & Eve

BY S. FRANCIS, H. DUGMORE & RICO

FWOOM!!

BRING THE MEAT. THE BRAAI'S READY.

MOM! WHAT HAPPENED?!

I SQUIRTED LIGHTER FLUID ON THE CHARCOAL.

ARE YOU CRAZY?! THAT'S DANGEROUS!!

NOW YOU TELL ME!

AND IF I WERE YOU, I'D GO TAKE A LOOK IN THE MIRROR.

AAAAAAH!!

ONE OF THOSE LITTLE MOMENTS THAT MAKE LIFE WORTH LIVING.

MADAM & Eve

BY S. FRANCIS, H. DUGMORE & RICO

HI! I'M EVE! CAN I GET YOU ANYTHING?

OF ALL THE DOMESTIC WORKERS IN THE WORLD, WE HAD TO GET ONE WHO PLAYS WITH PUPPETS.

GWEN! EVE'S PLAYING WITH PUPPETS AGAIN!

GWEN! EVE'S PLAYING WITH PUPPETS AGAIN!

HELP! HELP! LET GO OF ME!! CHOKE

GASP! I ...CAN'T BREATHE ...EVERYTHING'S GOING DARK. IT LOOKS LIKE I WASHED MY LAST DISH...CLEANED MY LAST WINDOW...

GOODBYE CRUEL WORLD... I'M HEADING FOR THE BIG WASHING MACHINE IN THE SKY!

PLOP!

FINALLY! ...AND GOOD RIDDANCE!

POLICE OFFICERS, MA'AM. WE'D LIKE TO ASK YOU A FEW QUESTIONS.

MADAM & Eve

BY S.FRANCIS, H.DUGMORE & RICO.

THERE'S AN INTERESTING **QUIZ** IN THE MAGAZINE THIS MONTH... IT'S CALLED... "HOW GOOD A MADAM ARE YOU?"

WHAT A WASTE OF TIME.

♫ CHICKEN... CLUCK CLUCK CLUCK CLUCK. ♫

OKAY. GO AHEAD.

QUESTION # 1: YOUR MAID ASKS YOU FOR A RAISE. YOU: ...

A-- GIVE IT TO HER; B-- DON'T GIVE IT TO HER; C-- IGNORE HER.

A-- GIVE IT TO HER.

MADAM...IT'S NO USE TAKING THIS QUIZ UNLESS YOU'RE HONEST.

I AM BEING HONEST! GO AHEAD... ASK ME FOR A RAISE!

CAN I HAVE A RAISE?

YES!! ....SEE?! I TOLD YOU I WAS BEING HONEST!

YOU'RE RIGHT! AND THANKS FOR THE RAISE, MADAM!

RIGHT. QUESTION #2: "PAID LEAVE..."

WAIT A MINUTE! LET ME SEE THAT "QUIZ."

HEY! THAT'S A CAR MAGAZINE!

UH-OH.

MADAM & Eve

BY S.FRANCIS, H.DUGMORE & RICO

YOU WANT ME TO HIRE YOU? WHAT DO YOU DO?

THIS! I'M VERY GOOD AT HOLDING A SIGN

YOUR ADVER-

BUT WHAT GOOD DOES THAT DO ME?

THINK OF THE POSSIBILITIES! SUPPOSE I STAND IN FRONT OF YOUR DRIVEWAY LIKE THIS--

YOUR A DVER.

THIS HOUSE PROTECTED BY ARMED RESPONSE

I ALREADY HAVE A SIGN THAT DOES THAT!

OH GREAT! REPLACED BY AUTOMATION!

THIS HOUSE PROTECTED BY ARMED RE.

OKAY-SUPPOSE I STAND IN FRONT OF YOUR HOUSE WITH THIS!

(YOUR STREET ADDRESS HERE)

NICE TRY. MY MAILBOX ALREADY DOES THAT.

OH, PERFECT! REPLACED BY A MAILBOX!!

IT'S NOT MY FAULT.

THINK! THERE MUST BE SOME WAY YOU CAN UTILISE MY SIGN-HOLDING TALENT!

WORK HARD

TIME IS MONEY

92

MADAM & Eve

BY S.FRANCIS, H.DUGMORE & RICO

MOM — ASK EVE TO GO TO THE CHEMIST. MY NOSE IS ALL STUFFY.

YOU ASK HER.

FINE! IF IT'S SUCH A BIG OPERATION, I'LL GO MYSELF!

MADAM'S GOING TO THE CHEMIST FOR HER STUFFED-UP NOSE. SHE SAYS IT'S SUCH A BIG OPERATION, SHE HAD TO GO HERSELF.

DID YOU HEAR ABOUT EVE'S MADAM?

NO. WHAT?

SHE'S GOING TO THE CHEMIST. HER NOSE IS STUFFED UP BECAUSE OF HER OPERATION.

DID YOU HEAR ABOUT EVE'S MADAM? SHE HAD A BIG OPERATION ON HER NOSE...

BUT THEY STUFFED IT UP!

REALLY?!

EVE'S MADAM IS HAVING ANOTHER OPERATION ON HER BIG NOSE. THEY STUFFED UP THE FIRST ONE.

GOOD LUCK WITH YOUR SECOND NOSE JOB, MRS ANDERSON.

TWAS THE NIGHT BEFORE CHRISTMAS AND AT THE NORTH POLE, FATHER CHRISTMAS WAS READY TO ROCK AND TO ROLL.

MADAM & Eve

BY S. FRANCIS, H. DUGMORE & RICO

HE CHECKED HIS EQUIPMENT, HE CHECKED OUT HIS SLEIGH; FOR SOON HE'D ARRIVE ON THE STREETS OF SA.

HE GOT SUITED UP. HE WAS UP FOR THE TEST.

AND IN CAME HIS ELVES WITH HIS BULLET-PROOF VEST.

HE'D BEEN THERE BEFORE... AND HE KNEW IT WAS VIOLENT.

...HE WAS HOPING HOWEVER, THAT TONIGHT WOULD BE SILENT.

HE REACHED THE FIRST TOWN AND LOOKED AT THE MAP. THE STREETS WERE ALL QUIET... COULD THIS BE A *TRAP*?!!

COVER ME. I'M GOING IN!

AND A MADAM AND MAID THEN HEARD SUCH A CLATTER... THEY AROSE FROM THEIR BEDS TO SEE WHAT WAS THE MATTER.

STANDARD FORMATION! MOVE! MOVE!

IS **THIS** WHAT IT'S COME TO?" EVE SAID WITH A GROAN. "FATHER CHRISTMAS DECKED OUT LIKE SYLVESTER STALLONE?!"

"YOU'RE RIGHT", SIGHED FC, "I GOT CARRIED AWAY. I EVEN PUT GUARD BARS ON TOP OF MY SLEIGH!"

"CHRISTMAS IS **JOYFUL** — WHY, THAT IS THE ESSENCE! SHOULD I BE **AFRAID** TO DELIVER MY PRESENTS?!"

"BOYS - DROP YOUR WEAPONS! THROW DOWN YOUR ROUNDS!

...AND LITTLE ELF UZIS FELL TO THE GROUND.

AND THEY HEARD HIM EXCLAIM AS HE DROVE OUT OF SIGHT-- "PEACE ON EARTH TO YOU ALL! MERRY CHRISTMAS, GOOD NIGHT!"

96

MADAM & EVE

BY S. FRANCIS, H. DUGMORE & RICO

HI, I'M BIG JAKE ... AND THIS IS WEASEL. WE'RE HERE TO TALK TO YOU ABOUT AN EXCITING NEW SERVICE BEING OFFERED IN YOUR COMMUNITY...

... HELL'S ANGELS ARMED RESPONSE.

WE STOPPED CRIME IN YEOVILLE ... AND NOW WE CAN DO THE SAME FOR YOU.

UH... HOW MUCH DOES IT COST?

ONLY A FEW BUCKS A DAY AND ALL THE BEER WE CAN DRINK.

I'M SORRY... BUT WE ALREADY HAVE AN ARMED RESPONSE SERVICE.

NOT ANYMORE. THOSE WIMPS LEFT TOWN MYSTERIOUSLY AFTER WE TOOK OVER THEIR OFFICES.

AND WAIT TILL YOU SEE OUR RESPONSE TIME! WEASEL, HIT THE BUTTON!!

BUZZ!!

GIVE 'EM A FEW MINUTES. THEY MIGHT BE MAKING A BEER RUN.

HEY! BIG JAKE!

BIG MAMMA!

... BIG MAMMA?

100

HELLO, TOKOLOSHE HEADQUARTERS? YEAH--FORGET **THIS** HOUSE. ALL THEIR BEDS ARE ON BRICKS. I'LL BE BACK SOON. LET'S DO BREAKFAST.

IS THERE **ANYONE** WHO DOESN'T HAVE A ☺☆#☺☆·‼# CELLPHONE THESE DAYS?‼

MADAM & EVE PRESENTS:
JACK AND THE BEANSTALK
1996

JACK--TAKE THIS COW TO MARKET AND SELL IT.

YES, MOTHER.

PSST. HEY KID-- WANT TO BUY SOME MAGIC BEANS?

OKAY. I'LL TRADE YOU THIS COW FROM ENGLAND.

ARE YOU CRAZY?!

FORGET THE WHOLE THING!!

☆ THE END. ☆

MADAM...THE WASHING MACHINE IS BROKEN.

SO? JUST DO ALL THE WASHING BY HAND.

CHOKE! YOU WANT ME TO DO THE WASHING BY HAND?!!

WHAT'S HER PROBLEM?

YOU'VE HEARD OF HOMOPHOBIA?

YES?

EVE SUFFERS FROM OMO-PHOBIA.

MADAM & Eve

BY S.FRANCIS, H.DUGMORE & RICO

AND IN OTHER NEWS... **RASTAFARIANS** EVERYWHERE HAVE THREATENED MASS ACTION TO BLOCK OFF ALL MAIN ROADS AND HIGHWAYS... IF THE GOVERNMENT DOESN'T **LEGALISE DAGGA** IMMEDIATELY.

GATHER ROUND EVERYBODY... STRATEGY SESSION! ...WE ARE **HERE**!

COUGH COUGH HOLD IT, MON! THAT'S A MAP OF ICELAND!

BUMMER.

WE'RE REPORTING **LIVE** FROM JOHANNESBURG... WHERE, IN A SEMI-ORGANISED PROTEST, THOUSANDS OF RASTAFARIANS ARE ATTEMPTING TO BLOCKADE CITY STREETS.

TELL ME... WHAT DO YOU CALL THIS PROTEST?

WE CALL IT-- ROLLING **MASS ACTION**, MON.

MEANING WHAT, EXACTLY?

SIMPLE! WHILE WE HAVE DE **MASS** ACTION, WE BE DOIN' LOTS OF ROLLING.

DE GOVERNMENT MUST LEGALISE DAGGA!!

COUGH COUGH

LEGALISE DAGGA!! LEGALISE DAGGA!! LEGALISE DAGGA!!

COUGH

RIGHT. COULD I ASK YOU ONE MORE QUESTION?

SURE 'TING, MON.

...ARE YOU AWARE YOU'RE BLOCKADING A DEAD-END STREET?

CUL DE SAC

HEY MON! DIS A DEAD-END STREET!!

NO PROBLEM, MON! WE JUST REMOVE DE SIGN! COUGH!

LEGALISE DAGGA!! LEGALISE DAGGA!! LEGALISE DAGGA!!

MADAM & Eve

BY S. FRANCIS, H. DUGMORE & RICO

WELL, THE FACTS ARE CLEAR. *SOMEONE* BROKE MY NEW VASE.

I HEREBY CONVENE THIS FAMILY TRUTH COMMISSION.

BANG!

OKAY. WHO WANTS TO TELL THE TRUTH FIRST?

I WILL. SHE DID IT. I SAW HER!

EVE? DO YOU HAVE ANYTHING TO SAY?

SIGH YES.

IT WAS I. I DID IT. I ACCIDENTALLY BROKE THE VASE.

EVE, YOU TOLD THE *TRUTH!* I'M PROUD OF YOU. AND NOW, IT'S TIME FOR RECONCILIATION.

...YOU OWE ME R 29.95.

WHAT?!

I'M DEDUCTING R 29.95 FROM YOUR WAGES. NOW WE'RE RECONCILED.

WHAT ABOUT ME? I TOLD THE *TRUTH* TOO!

RIGHT. HERE'S YOUR *COMMISSION.* ...TEN BUCKS.

I HEREBY ANNOUNCE THIS TRUTH AND RECONCILIATION COMMISSION CLOSED!

BANG!!

SOMEHOW, I THINK SOMETHING GOT *LOST* IN THE TRANSLATION.

105

MADAM...

WHO'S THAT?

THIS IS THE TRUTH COMMISSION. YOU ARE CHARGED WITH TAKING ADVANTAGE OF YOUR DOMESTIC WORKER. HOW DO YOU PLEAD?

WAIT! I DEMAND MY RIGHT TO LEGAL COUNSEL!

PRESENT, YOUR HONOUR!

SORRY I'M LATE, MADAM.

I MOVE FOR A RECESS WHILE I REVIVE MY CLIENT.

GRANTED.

THIS TRUTH COMMISSION DEMANDS THAT YOU GIVE US THE TRUE FACTS REGARDING YOUR DOMESTIC WORKER'S EMPLOYMENT!

ALRIGHT! ALRIGHT! I ADMIT IT! FOR YEARS AND YEARS I'VE PAID MY MAID ONLY 10 RAND A DAY!

I SEE...

IS SHE AVAILABLE TUESDAYS?

THE TRUTH COMMISSION CONTINUES...

EXHIBIT A, YOUR HONOUR -- A PAIR OF HOUSEHOLD RUBBER GLOVES. I WILL NOW ASK MY CLIENT TO PUT THEM ON.

I... CAN'T. THEY'RE TOO SMALL.

...THEY'RE TOO SMALL!

SO WHAT? THAT JUST PROVES SHE NEVER WASHED ANY DISHES.

NICE MOVE, JOHNNIE COCHRAN.

I CAN'T UNDERSTAND IT... IT WORKED FOR O.J. SIMPSON.

YOUR HONOUR... MAY I SUBMIT TO THE TRUTH COMMISSION EXHIBITS B, C AND D.

HAIR SAMPLES, CARPET SCRAPINGS AND ASSORTED FIBRES.

PROVING WHAT?

...PROVING THAT I VACUUM ON A REGULAR BASIS.

YOUR HONOUR! I WISH TO FIRE MY LAWYER!!

NO WAY. WE LIKE HER.

...AND I SUBMIT TO THE TRUTH COMMISSION THAT MY CLIENT NEVER MEANT TO UNDERPAY ME.

LOOK AT THIS FACE. IS THIS THE FACE OF SOMEONE THAT WOULD TAKE ADVANTAGE OF A DOMESTIC WORKER?

ON SECOND THOUGHT, CAN WE STRIKE THAT FROM THE RECORD?

GOOD IDEA.

THIS TRUTH COMMISSION IS NOW IN SESSION. IS COUNSEL READY?

READY, YOUR HONOUR.

GWEN ANDERSON... YOU ARE CHARGED WITH UNDER-PAYING YOUR DOMESTIC WORKER. HOW DO YOU PLEAD?

GUILTY WITH AN EXPLANATION, YOUR HONOUR.

WHAT'S THE EXPLANATION?

SHE'S CHEAP.

HEY!!

A QUIET RURAL VILLAGE, SOUTH OF THE LIMPOPO.

SUDDENLY, THE SILENCE IS BROKEN... BY TWO DOZEN SPEEDING LIMOUSINES...

WHAT IS IT, MOMMY?! IS **MADIBA** COMING?!

NO... IT'S **SARAFINA II**!!

LOOK MOMMY! ...HELICOPTERS!

OKAY, EVERYONE. THIS IS THE PLACE. LAND THE HELICOPTERS AND PARK THE AIR CONDITIONED BUSES!

HEY, KID. WE'RE THE **SARAFINA II** TOURING COMPANY. WHERE'S YOUR **THEATRE**?

THEATRE? THIS IS A SMALL VILLAGE. WE DON'T HAVE A THEATRE.

NO PROBLEM, KID. WE'LL BUILD ONE.

HEY! SOMEBODY GET ME THE CHEQUEBOOK!!

WE FORGOT TO BRING IT, SIR. CAN WE USE PETTY CASH?

THE CAST OF SARAFINA II ARRIVES...

THE LIMO RIDE WAS EXHAUSTING! WHERE'S MY PRIVATE DRESSING ROOM?!

WE'RE BUILDING THEM NOW.

AGAIN?! ...EVERY SMALL VILLAGE WE GO TO, IT'S THE SAME THING!! ...**NO DRESSING ROOMS!!**

I'VE **HAD** IT! IF ANYONE WANTS ME, I'LL BE WATCHING VIDEOS IN MY AIR CONDITIONED BUS!!

THESE PEOPLE IN THE CHORUS LINE THINK THEY'RE SOOOO SPECIAL.

THE **SARAFINA II** CATERERS HAVE ARRIVED, SIR. HERE'S TODAY'S WINE LIST.

ABOUT TIME!

WOW, MISTER! BRINGING THIS PLAY TO MY VILLAGE MUST HAVE COST A **LOT** OF MONEY!

MONEY?!! YOU THINK THIS IS **ABOUT** MONEY?!! ...THIS IS ABOUT BRINGING AN IMPORTANT **HEALTH** MESSAGE TO THE PEOPLE!!

HEY-- IF I TOLD EVERY-ONE THE MESSAGE, THEN WHO'D PAY TWENTY BUCKS A TICKET?!

WHAT MESSAGE?

THANK YOU FOR INVITING MY SON TO THE **SARAFINA II** CAST PARTY, SIR.

HEY--NO PROBLEM! WE HAVE THEM **EVERY** NIGHT. BESIDES... I LIKE THE KID.

SO, DID YOU ENJOY THE SHOW, KID?

YES, SIR.

AND REMEMBER ...YOU'LL BE GETTING OLDER SOON, ...SO I HOPE SARAFINA II TAUGHT YOU A VALUABLE LESSON.

YES SIR...

...ALWAYS GET A **GOVERNMENT SUBSIDY**.

RIGHT ON, KID. WANT SOME CAVIAR?

MADAM & EVE

BY S. FRANCIS, H. DUGMORE & RICO

TODAY'S TOP STORY-- PRESIDENT NELSON MANDELA ENTERED THE PARK LANE CLINIC THIS WEEK FOR A ROUTINE PHYSICAL.

ISN'T THAT THE **SAME** HOSPITAL YOUR MOTHER WENT TO FOR HER ANNUAL CHECK-UP?

YOU'RE **SURE** YOU DON'T WANT A GIN & TONIC, MISTER PRESIDENT?

NURSE!

WAIT TILL MY FRIENDS FIND OUT I WAS IN THE SAME HOSPITAL ROOM AS NELSON MANDELA!

;SIGH;

BY THE WAY... I LOVE YOUR HOSPITAL GOWN. IS IT BY THE SAME GUY WHO DESIGNS ALL YOUR **SHIRTS**?

YES.

GOOD. FOR A SECOND THERE, I THOUGHT IT WAS THE **MEDICATION** I'M TAKING.

PLEASE. I REALLY NEED TO REST.

SO. WHAT DO YOU THINK OF **WINNIE'S** NEW LOOK?

PARDON ME?

I KNOW! LET'S HAVE SOME **FUN** WITH THE DOCTORS! LET'S **SWITCH** MEDICAL CHARTS!

NURSE!!

HEY!! WHAT ARE YOU DOING OUT OF BED?!

UH-OH. IT'S NURSE RATCHED.

AND IN FINANCIAL NEWS, THE **RAND** TOOK A NOSEDIVE TODAY, FOLLOWING THE ANNOUNCEMENT BY DOCTORS...

...THAT NELSON MANDELA HAS THE BODY OF A SHORT 82 YEAR-OLD WOMAN...

AND IN OTHER NEWS, PLANS ARE UNDERWAY TO BUILD A GIANT STATUE AT A COST OF 50 MILLION RAND.

THE BRONZE STATUE, ONE OF THE LARGEST IN THE WORLD, WILL BE A LIKENESS OF NELSON MANDELA'S...

... HAND.

JUST MY HAND?! THAT'S ALL?!

IT'S VERY RECOGNISABLE, SIR.

AND TODAY'S TOP STORY... SCULPTORS BEGAN WORK TODAY ON THE GIANT STATUE OF NELSON MANDELA'S HAND.

CAN I HELP YOU?

YES. I'M HERE TO SEE THE PRESIDENT.

YOU'LL HAVE TO WAIT. THE PRESIDENT'S BUSY POSING FOR HIS STATUE.

I'M GETTING TIRED. CAN I TAKE A BREAK?

SORRY, SIR. THE PINKY'S VERY TRICKY.

MISTER PRESIDENT... THE PRODUCER OF SARAFINA II IS HERE TO SEE YOU.

SHOW HIM IN.

JUST HEAR ME OUT, MISTER PRESIDENT. SURE, YOU COULD SPEND 50 MILLION RAND ON A GIANT STATUE OF YOUR HAND.

OR,... YOU COULD INVEST THE MONEY IN A NEW MUSICAL CALLED HAND-A-FINA!!

NOT JUST ENTERTAINMENT, BUT FULL OF HEALTH MESSAGES. THE DANGERS OF NAIL-BITING...

I'M CALLING SECURITY.

120

MISTER PRESIDENT... COULD WE TALK TO YOU FOR A MOMENT?

OF COURSE.

NOW THAT THE **GIANT STATUE** OF YOUR **HAND** IS ALMOST FINISHED...

WE WERE WONDERING IF WE COULD MOVE IT SOMEWHERE ELSE.

WHY?

I DON'T KNOW, SIR. IT MAKES ME A LITTLE NERVOUS.

AND IN OTHER NEWS, THE 50 MILLION RAND **STATUE** OF NELSON MANDELA'S **HAND** WAS FINALLY COMPLETED TODAY...

ALTHOUGH, **WHERE** THE PRESIDENT WILL DECIDE TO EXHIBIT THE STATUE, STILL REMAINS A MYSTERY.

GOOD MORNING, **MRS. MANDELA.** WOULD YOU LIKE BREAKFAST IN BED?

YES. OPEN THE CURTAINS.

AAAAH!

MADAM & Eve TAKES A LOOK AT OTHER CELEBRITY GIANT HAND STATUES.

BRUCE LEE

CAPTAIN HOOK

SARAFINA II

121

MADAM & Eve

LADIES AND GENTLEMEN, THANK YOU FOR COMING TO THE LAUNCH OF THE GOVERNMENT'S TOP SECRET NEW WEAPON... YOU'VE HEARD OF WATER DIVINERS AND WITCH-FINDERS... WELL, WE'VE TAKEN IT ONE STEP FURTHER!

BY S. FRANCIS, H. DUGMORE & RICO

A RACIST-SNIFFER.

A DOG?

WHY NOT? DOGS CAN BE TRAINED TO SNIFF OUT DRUGS... BOMBS... WHY NOT RACISTS?

THINK OF WHAT IT WILL MEAN TO THE COUNTRY! FROM NOW ON, WE CAN CONCLUSIVELY DETERMINE WHO'S A RACIST... AND WHO ISN'T.

LET ME DEMONSTRATE. GO, RUSTY! GO... FIND A RACIST!!

SNIFF. SNIFF.

WOOF! WOOF! WOOF! WOOF! WOOF!

LADIES AND GENTLEMEN!! ...WE'VE FOUND THE RACIST!

CLAP! CLAP! CLAP! CLAP! CLAP! CLAP! CLAP! CLAP! CLAP!

NOT SO FAST! I HAD A ROAST BEEF SANDWICH FROM THE BUFFET IN MY POCKET!!

BAD DOG! DON'T YOU KNOW THE DIFFERENCE BETWEEN A RACIST AND A ROAST BEEF SANDWICH?!

THAT'S OKAY. NEITHER DOES BARNEY PITYANA.

I'M NOT TAKING THIS LYING DOWN!

TODAY'S TOP STORY... AN EMERGENCY MEETING OF PARLIAMENT WAS CONVENED THIS WEEK TO DECIDE ONE OF THE MOST IMPORTANT ISSUES THE NEW SOUTH AFRICA HAS FACED YET...

LADIES & GENTLEMEN... WE'RE HOPELESSLY DEADLOCKED... AND TIME IS RUNNING OUT. WE'VE **GOT** TO MAKE A DECISION!

SO, UNLESS THERE IS AN OBJECTION. I SAY WE VOTE AGAIN.

ALL THOSE IN FAVOUR OF **DENZEL WASHINGTON** AS NELSON MANDELA IN "LONG WALK TO FREEDOM," RAISE YOUR HAND.

NO WAY!! SIDNEY POITIER!!

I'M TELLING YOU, MR. PRESIDENT--THIS "LONG WALK TO FREEDOM" MOVIE COULD BE A BOXOFFICE BLOCKBUSTER! ...ACADAMY AWARD CITY!

PICTURE IT: SIDNEY POITIER AS **YOU**... MICHAEL CAINE AS FW DE KLERK...

AND GET THIS: FOR **WINNIE**... WE'RE TALKING TO WHOOPI GOLDBERG!

SHE'S INTERESTED?!

ONLY IF SHE DOESN'T HAVE TO WEAR THAT HAT.

MR PRESIDENT... I'LL BE HONEST. WE'RE A LITTLE WORRIED ABOUT THE "LONG WALK TO FREEDOM" MOVIE.

NOW WHAT'S THE PROBLEM?

THE ENDING! WE NEED TO CONCLUDE YOUR LIFE STORY WITH SOMETHING BIG!

SOMETHING BIG??

WAIT A MINUTE... I'VE GOT IT!! THE PARLIAMENT CATCHES **FIRE**...

...AND YOU CARRY THE MP'S OUT ON YOUR BACK!!

ALL OF THEM?!!

LET ME COME STRAIGHT TO THE POINT, CHIEF BUTHELEZI: WE NEED YOUR HELP ON THE "LONG WALK TO FREEDOM" MOVIE.

EVEN THOUGH IT'S A TRUE STORY... WE NEED A BIG ENDING! SOMETHING TO REALLY "WOW" THE AUDIENCE.

I'VE GOT IT!! THE IFP IS GRANTED INTERNATIONAL MEDIATION, BECOMES A MAJORITY VOICE IN THE NEW CONSTITUTION....AND IS AWARDED KWA-ZULU NATAL AS AN INDEPENDENT STATE WITH ME AS PRESIDENT FOR LIFE.

REMEMBER SIR, OUR BUDGET DOESN'T ALLOW FOR SPECIAL EFFECTS.

TRUST ME, CHIEF BUTHELEZI. THE "LONG WALK TO FREEDOM" MOVIE NEEDS A BIG ENDING! PICTURE IT: YOU AND MADIBA SHAKE HANDS, SOLVE ALL YOUR PROBLEMS, AND WALK INTO THE SUNSET.

WHAT?!! YOU WANT ME TO PUT ASIDE MY DIFFERENCES AND SELL OUT MY OWN PARTY--- JUST SO YOUR MOVIE CAN HAVE A HAPPY ENDING?!!

WE'LL GIVE YOU A PERCENTAGE OF THE GROSS.

ARE WE TALKING VIDEO RENTALS AND SALES TO TELEVISION?

CHIEF... YOU DRIVE A HARD BARGAIN.

URK.

THAT'S IT! YOU GOT HER!!

BONK!

YOU WERE RIGHT, MADAM. I NEVER REALISED HOW MUCH FUN WOMEN'S SELF-DEFENCE CLASSES ARE.

HOOOOH!! YEOOOOO.!!

WHOOOOHA!! HOOOOO!!

WHO DO YOU THINK YOU ARE·· BRUCE LEE?

NO. THE FLOOR'S COLD.

BOY, THIS WOMEN'S SELF·DEFENCE INSTRUCTOR IS REALLY STRICT.

ARE YOU TALKING IN CLASS?!

DROP DOWN AND GIVE ME TWENTY!!

PUSH-UPS, MADAM. SHE MEANS TWENTY PUSH-UPS.

THIS SELF-DEFENCE CLASS IS PATHETIC! NOT ONE OF YOU HAS HAD ANY PREVIOUS TRAINING IN MARTIAL ARTS!

THAT'S NOT TRUE! I'M A MASTER OF "GO-SHIN."

"GO-SHIN"? WHAT'S THAT?

WHACK!!!

WHEN IN DOUBT, ALWAYS GO FOR THE SHIN.

#☆#6!!#

YOU CALL YOURSELVES SELF-DEFENCE STUDENTS?! THIS WAS THE WORST CLASS I EVER TAUGHT!!

NOW GO HIT THE SHOWERS!!

HEYA!! HEEYA!! HAI!!

MARGE... THAT'S A LOVELY KARATE BELT.

THANK YOU. I GOT IT AT THAT NEW BOUTIQUE.

YOURS IS NICE ALSO. IS IT PLAID?

YOU LIKE IT? I BOUGHT A MATCHING HEADBAND, TOO.

OOH. IS THAT SILK?

KUGEL-FU.

ARE THOSE NEW SANDALS?

MADAM & Eve

MADAM & Eve presents:

UPCOMING 14 MILLION RAND MUSICALS

...WITH AN EDUCATIONAL MESSAGE.

BY S. FRANCIS, H. DUGMORE & RICO

PARAFFINA

INSTRUCTS THE SAFE USE OF PARAFFIN AND FIRE PREVENTION.

SAHARAFINA

TEACHES ABOUT THE HAZARDS OF GETTING LOST IN THE DESERT.

LAVAFINA

WARNS OF THE DANGERS OF LIVING TOO CLOSE TO AN ACTIVE VOLCANO.

HIJACKAFINA

IMPARTS SAFETY TIPS FOR MOTORISTS IN EXPENSIVE CARS.

SARAFINA-II-FINA

TEACHES POLITICIANS THE WISDOM OF SPENDING 14 MILLION ON AN EDUCATIONAL MUSICAL.

MADAM & Eve

BY S. FRANCIS, H. DUGMORE & RICO

MADAM & EVE PRESENTS:

EXPEDITION TO TERROR

"IT ALL STARTED INNOCENTLY ENOUGH... A MAJOR SUNDAY NEWSPAPER SPONSORED OUR CLIMBING EXPEDITION TO THE HIMALAYAS..."

"ONLY THE MOST *EXPERIENCED* CLIMBERS WERE HAND-PICKED FOR OUR *NON-RACIAL* TEAM."

ONE TIME, I TOOK THE LIFT TO THE TOP OF THE CARLTON CENTRE.

YOU'RE ACCEPTED.

"OUR EXPEDITION LEADER SEEMED NICE ENOUGH..."

DRESS WARMLY, GUYS. IT'S COLD UP THERE.

"... IF YOU LEARNED TO IGNORE HIS SUDDEN *MOOD SWINGS*..."

KILL! I'LL KILL YOU ALL!

AN INTREPID *JOURNALIST* ACCOMPANIED US TO RECORD OUR PROGRESS."

THE REPORTER IS DANGLING FROM A CLIFF, SIR.

GOOD. IT'LL TEACH HIM A LESSON.

HELP!

"WORD OF OUR HARDSHIPS REACHED THE SPONSORING NEWSPAPER..."

ACCORDING TO REPORTS, THE NON-RACIAL TEAM IS FREEZING, INEXPERIENCED, DISORGANISED ... AND THE LEADER'S A PSYCHOPATH. DO YOU REALISE WHAT THIS MEANS?

YES.

IT'S A PUBLIC RELATIONS DISASTER.

"MIRACULOUSLY, WE FINALLY REACHED THE SUMMIT OF *MOUNT EVEREST*..."

I PLANT THIS FLAG IN THE NAME OF SOUTH AFRICA!!

UH, SIR? I THINK YOU ACCIDENTALLY IMPALED ONE OF THE CLIMBERS.

DAMN. IT'S NOT THE BLACK GIRL, IS IT?

DON'T MISS OUR NEXT THRILL-PACKED EPISODE —

MUTINY IN THE HIMALAYAS

Panel 1: SILHOUETTED AGAINST THE SLOPES OF MOUNT EVEREST: A SMALL GROUP OF CLIMBERS...

Panel 2: WHO **ARE** THESE COURAGEOUS EXPLORERS... THAT **LAUGH** IN THE FACE OF **DANGER**?

Panel 3: ... A NON-RACIAL, NON-SEXIST GROUP OF PROFESSIONALS SPONSORED BY A MAJOR SUNDAY NEWSPAPER?

Panel 4: NO! IT'S THE **MADAM & EVE** MOUNTAIN CLIMBING EXPEDITION!

EVE! GET OFF!! YOU'RE STANDING ON MY FACE!!

Panel 5: SLOWLY... RELENTLESSLY... THE MADAM & EVE MOUNTAIN EXPEDITION PRESSES ON...

Panel 6: WHEN SUDDENLY...

BOING!

Panel 7: HOO! HOO!

Panel 8: GREAT. MAD YAK DISEASE.

Panel 9: LOOK OVER THERE! THERE'S **ANOTHER** GROUP OF MOUNTAIN CLIMBERS... AND THEY'RE FROM SOUTH AFRICA.

Panel 10: HELLO THERE!! WE'RE FROM SOUTH AFRICA TOO! COME OVER AND JOIN US FOR TEA!!

Panel 11:

MADAM & Eve

BY S. FRANCIS, H. DUGMORE & RICO

AS PRESIDENT OF THE NEW SOUTH AFRICA... I SAY SHOUT IT FROM THE ROOFTOPS! WE'RE FREE-- WE'RE FREE AT...AT...

DAMN. WHAT'S THE LINE AGAIN?

"LAST," MR. POITIER. "FREE AT LAST."

CUT!!

SID. BABE. YOU SEEM TO BE HAVING A LITTLE TROUBLE.

SORRY. IT'S THAT LINE! IT JUST DOESN'T ROLL OFF MY TONGUE.

HEY. NO PROBLEM! WE'LL CHANGE IT.

HOW ABOUT THIS-- "SHOUT IT FROM THE ROOFTOPS! WE'RE FREE-- AND IT'S ABOUT TIME!!"

UH...

WAIT A MINUTE! I GOT IT!! "SO SHOUT IT FROM THE ROOFTOPS-- WE'RE FREE-- AND BOY, DOES IT FEEL GOOD!!

HMMM.

EXCUSE ME, SIR..."FREE AT LAST" IS PART OF HISTORY. YOU CAN'T JUST "CHANGE" IT-- IN FACT, IT'S ONE OF THE MOST FAMOUS THINGS NELSON MANDELA'S EVER SAID.

OF COURSE!! IT'S A CATCHPHRASE! LIKE EASTWOOD'S "MAKE MY DAY"... OR SCHWARZENEGGER'S "HASTA LA VISTA, BABY."

SIDNEY - THE KID'S RIGHT. THIS "FREE AT LAST" THING COULD BE BIG. LET'S LEAVE IT IN.

GOOD THINKING.

...AND ACTION!!

SHOUT IT FROM THE ROOFTOPS! WE'RE FREE AT LAST!

DON'T YOU JUST LOVE WATCHING THE HOLLYWOOD CREATIVE PROCESS?

YOU'RE NOT GOING TO BELIEVE THIS, MOM. EVE GOT A **SMALL ROLE** IN THE NEW MANDELA-DE KLERK **MOVIE** THEY'RE FILMING HERE.

EVE IN A MOVIE? WHAT DOES SHE DO?

SHE PLAYS THE PART OF A LOYAL AND HARD-WORKING DOMESTIC WORKER.

SHE PULLS THAT ONE OFF, IT COULD MEAN AN ACADEMY AWARD.

I HEARD THAT!!

REMEMBER, EVE, IN THIS SCENE, YOU'LL BE SERVING THE PRESIDENT TEA. YOU WALK IN, SAY YOUR LINE, AND WALK OUT.

NO PROBLEM.

DIRECTOR

QUIET ON THE SET! ...AND... *ACTION!!*

WOULD YOU LIKE SOME TEA, MISTER PRESIDENT?

SIDNEY POITIER!! I LOVE YOU!!

CUT!!

WOULD YOU LIKE SOME **TEA**, MISTER PRESIDENT?

WOULD **YOU** LIKE SOME TEA, MISTER PRESIDENT?

WOULD YOU **LIKE** SOME TEA, MISTER **PRESIDENT**?

WOULD YOU LIKE... **SOME TEA MISTER** PRESIDENT?

QUIET PLEASE! AND... *ACTION!*

WOULD YOU LIKE SOME PRESIDENT, MISTER TEA?

CUT.

BY S.FRANCIS, H.DUGMORE & RICO

138

MADAM & Eve

BY S. FRANCIS, H. DUGMORE & RICO

One day, **Chicken Little** was hit on the head by a falling coin.

BONK!

DEAR ME! THE RAND IS FALLING! I MUST TELL KING NELSON.

On the way, **Chicken Little** met Ducky Lucky and Goosey Lucy...

WHERE ARE YOU GOING, CHICKEN LITTLE?

THE RAND IS FALLING. I MUST GO AND TELL KING NELSON!

THEN WE WILL GO WITH YOU.

And so, Chicken Little, Ducky Lucky and Goosey Lucy --

HOLD IT!!

IT'S BAD ENOUGH WE HAVE TO ACT OUT THIS STUPID PARABLE -- BUT TO DO IT DRESSED UP AS BIRDS?!

I DRAW THE LINE AT WEARING FEATHERS AND BEAKS! COUNT ME OUT!

And so, Ducky Lucky went on Strike.

SHE'S RIGHT. THIS IS STUPID.

And so, everyone else went on strike.

...which made the Rand fall EVEN MORE.

And the moral of the story... If you want to help save the Rand, Going on Strike is for the Birds.

OH, GIVE IT A REST!!

DEFINITELY THE MOST RIDICULOUS CARTOON I'VE EVER BEEN IN.

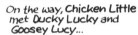

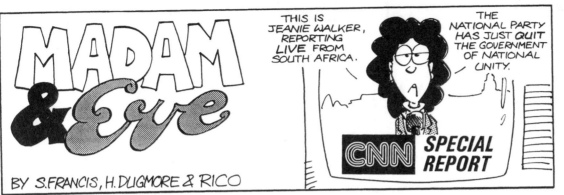

MADAM & Eve

BY S. FRANCIS, H. DUGMORE & RICO

THIS IS JEANIE WALKER, REPORTING LIVE FROM SOUTH AFRICA.

THE NATIONAL PARTY HAS JUST **QUIT** THE GOVERNMENT OF NATIONAL UNITY.

CNN **SPECIAL REPORT**

IT'S COMPLETE AND UTTER CHAOS! HUNDREDS OF NATIONAL PARTY MEMBERS HAVE CLIMBED TO THE TOP OF THE UNION BUILDINGS TO WAIT FOR THE **EVACUATING** HELICOPTERS!

NOT SINCE THE FALL OF SAIGON HAS THERE BEEN -- WAIT A MINUTE! HERE COME THE CHOPPERS!

THUK THUK THUK THUK THUK THUK

THUK THUK THUK THUK THUK

JEANIE-- WHAT ABOUT EX-DEPUTY PRESIDENT FW DE KLERK?

BOB... AS I UNDERSTAND IT, MR. DE KLERK HAS ALREADY BEEN WHISKED TO SAFETY IN A PRIVATE AIRPLANE.

AND THERE GOES THE LAST HELICOPTER! THERE'S STILL NATS WHO DIDN'T GET OUT!

WILL THEY BE TRAPPED FOREVER... BEHIND HOSTILE LINES IN AN ANC-DOMINATED GOVERNMENT?!

BUT WAIT! HERE COMES... RAMBO!!

THUK! THUK! THUK! THUK!

YO! GRAB MY HAND!!

HELP ME, RAMBO! HELP ME!

I THINK YOUR MOTHER'S HAVING A NIGHTMARE, MADAM.

HEY LOOK! THE RAND STABILISED.

HEY! WHAT HAPPENED TO MY GIN & TONIC?!

IF YOU ever want TO see your GIN & TONIC again, tell me a STORY.

ONCE UPON A TIME, THERE WAS A LITTLE GIRL WHO DIDN'T REALISE SHE WAS IN MORTAL DANGER...

WAIT! LET ME PULL UP A CHAIR!

ONCE UPON A TIME... THERE WAS A PLACE CALLED CAMELOT... AND KING ARTHUR USED TO SIT AT THE ROUND TABLE WITH HIS KNIGHTS.

BUT THEN MANY OF HIS WISEST KNIGHTS DECIDED TO FOOLISHLY LEAVE THE ROUND TABLE AND FORM AN OPPOSITION PARTY.

...INVESTOR CONFIDENCE WAS SHAKEN AND CAMELOT TURNED INTO A BANANA REPUBLIC. ...THE END!!

SLAM!

SHE'S STILL UPSET ABOUT THE NATS.

... AND GOLDILOCKS SAID: "THIS BED IS TOO SMALL!"

"AND THIS BED IS TOO HARD."

... AND THEN GOLDILOCKS SAID: "THIS BED IS JUST RIGHT."

... AND THAT'S WHY MADONNA'S PREGNANT.

MOM!!

142

CHUGGA CHUGGA.
CHUGGA CHUGGA.
TOOT! TOOT!

I THINK I CAN!
I THINK I CAN!
I KNOW I CAN!
I KNOW I CAN!

NOW GIVE ME LOTS
OF MONEY AND
CONSULTANCY
FEES!! ...THE END.

WHAT
STORY IS
THAT?

"THE LITTLE
GRAVY TRAIN
THAT COULD."

AND SO, DOROTHY
MET THE SCARECROW,
THE LION AND
THE TINMAN   OZ?
IN THE   IS THAT
LAND OF   IN SOUTH
OZ.   AFRICA?

YES. IT'S...UH,
SOMEWHERE OVER
THE RAINBOW
NATION.

HEE-HEE! GET IT?!
...SOMEWHERE OVER THE
RAINBOW NATION!!

...OVER THE
RAINBOW NATION!!
HEE-HEE!
HOO-HOO!   THESE
HAHAHA!   STORIES
              ALWAYS GET
              STRANGER
              AFTER TWO
              GIN & TONICS.

MADAM & Eve

BY S. FRANCIS, H. DUGMORE & RICO

I FIGURED IT OUT, LIZEKA. NOW I KNOW WHY I'VE BEEN HAVING SUCH **BAD LUCK** LATELY.

SOMEONE'S PUT A **CURSE** ON ME!

COME ON, ERIC. DON'T BE RIDICULOUS.

ERIC?

MEN WORKING

NOW DO YOU BELIEVE ME?

YOU THINK EVERYTHING THAT'S HAPPENED LATELY -- GETTING BURGLED..., THE FALLING RAND... MY INABILITY TO FIND A JOB... IT'S ALL COINCIDENCE?!!

GO AHEAD -- BE SCEPTICAL! I'M TELLING YOU -- I'VE BEEN **CURSED**!!

OKAY, OKAY. CALM DOWN.

OOPS! **LOOK OUT BELOW**!!

CRASH!!

LIZEKA -- ARE YOU OKAY?!

ERIC!! THINK ABOUT IT! THAT CEMENT BRICK COULD HAVE HIT YOU -- BUT IT DIDN'T!

DON'T YOU SEE WHAT THIS **MEANS**?! YOUR BAD LUCK IS GONE! THE CURSE IS BROKEN!!

BY THE WAY, YOUR CAR'S INSURED, ISN'T IT?

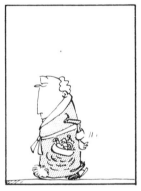

Panel 1: EVE! I JUST WOKE UP... AND I'M GOING TO NEED *LOTS* OF ATTENTION. / WHAT'S WRONG?

Panel 2: OHHHH. MY HEAD. MY THROAT. MY NOSE. MY JOINTS.

Panel 3: EVE-- I JUST WOKE UP. OHHHHH... MY HEAD. MY THROAT. MY NOSE. MY JOINTS.

Panel 4: SAME HERE. OHHHH. MY HEAD. MY THROAT. MY NOSE. MY JOINTS. / NICE TRY. JUST GET THE ASPIRIN.

Panel 5: BOY, AM I *SICK*. / YOU THINK *YOU'RE* SICK?! YOU SHOULD SEE HOW I FEEL!

Panel 6: AG, DOES MY HEAD HURT! / *YOUR* HEAD?! ...*MY* HEAD!

Panel 7: AG, MY JOINTS ACHE. / *YOUR* JOINTS?! ...*MY* JOINTS!

Panel 8: MY NOSE IS STUFFED. *YOUR* NOSE IS STUFFED?! WHAT ABOUT *MY* NOSE?! / DUELLING HYPO-CHONDRIACS.

Panel 9: OH, AM I *SICK*. AND OH, AM I *THIRSTY*. / NOT AS THIRSTY AS I AM.

Panel 10: OH, *AM I* THIRSTY. *NOT* AS THIRSTY AS I AM. / OKAY! OKAY! I BROUGHT YOU BOTH SOME WATER!!

Panel 11: (no dialogue)

Panel 12: OH, *WAS* I THIRSTY. / NOT AS THIRSTY AS *I* WAS.

147

MADAM & EVE

BY S. FRANCIS, H. DUGMORE & RICO

WELCOME TO TALK RADIO'S "TELL IT LIKE IT IS!" MY GUESTS IN THE STUDIO ARE GWEN AND ABIGAIL ANDERSON.

OUR SHOW TONIGHT-- "WHITE RACISTS WHO COME OUT OF THE CLOSET!!"

...AND WE'LL BE RIGHT BACK AFTER THIS COMMERCIAL MESSAGE.

...EXCUSE ME. WE WERE TOLD THE SUBJECT OF THE SHOW IS... "SHOPPING MALLS IN THE NEW SOUTH AFRICA."

IT IS! BUT A LITTLE CONTROVERSY ALWAYS HELPS MY POPULARITY RATINGS.

...TWO SECONDS!

AND WE'RE BACK! IF YOU JUST JOINED US, MY GUESTS TONIGHT ARE GWEN AND ABIGAIL ANDERSON...TWO LADIES WHO FREQUENTLY GO TO SHOPPING MALLS...

...SHOPPING MALLS WHERE LIBERAL WHITE RACISTS SECRETLY PLOT CONSPIRACIES TO BRING DOWN THE GOVERNMENT!!

I HAVE JUST ONE WORD TO SAY TO BOTH OF YOU-- WHITE RACISM! GO AHEAD-- TRY AND DENY IT!!

WHAT PART DID THESE TWO WHITE WOMEN PLAY IN THE RACIST CONSPIRACY TO BRING DOWN WILLIAM MAKGOBA AT WITS UNIVERSITY?! WE'LL FIND OUT-- AFTER THIS BRIEF COMMERCIAL MESSAGE.

YOU'RE DOING FINE, LADIES. WOULD YOU LIKE SOME TEA OR COFFEE?

THIS IS GWEN AND ABIGAIL ANDERSON. TONIGHT'S SHOW: "RADIO TALKSHOW HOSTS WITH CANES THAT HAVE TO BE SURGICALLY REMOVED." AND WE'LL BE RIGHT BACK AFTER THIS MESSAGE.

 栗!!

 PLINK PLINK

 NOW I KNOW WHY SHE PAID FOR MY KARATE LESSONS.

 HOLD IT!! THIS IS A STICK-UP! GIVE ME ALL YOUR MONEY!!

 HOOOAH!! YEOOOO!!

 KEEYAII!!

 SEE? THOSE WOMEN'S SELF-DEFENCE CLASSES REALLY PAID OFF.

MADAM & Eve

BY S. FRANCIS, H. DUGMORE & RICO

SO TAKE ADVANTAGE OF THE *OLYMPIC SPIRIT.* GO FOR THE *GOLD!*

BUY GOLD & SHINE FLOOR WAX. AUGH!

I CAN'T TAKE IT ANYMORE!! THEY'RE USING THE OLYMPICS TO MOTIVATE *EVERYTHING!*

EVE! YES, MADAM?

EVE! YOU'VE GOT TO CATCH THE OLYMPIC SPIRIT! BE ALL THAT YOU CAN BE!

GIVE IT YOUR BEST SHOT! GO FOR THE GOLD! GO FOR THE **GOLD**, EVE!

THANKS FOR REMINDING ME. YOU FORGOT TO PAY ME THIS MONTH.

OLYMPIC METAPHORS. THEY'RE SO TRICKY.

DR. ZUMA... IS IT TRUE YOU'VE FOUND A **MYSTERY DONOR** THAT HAS PROMISED TO FUND **SARAFINA II**?

YES.

BUT MINISTER... SOME PEOPLE BELIEVE THERE IS **NO REAL MYSTERY DONOR.**

NO MYSTERY DONOR?!

...THEN WHO'S **THIS**?!!

CAN WE ASK HIM QUESTIONS?

NO. BUT HE HAS A PREPARED MYSTERY STATEMENT.

DR. ZUMA-- CAN YOU REVEAL THE SECRET IDENTITY OF YOUR **MYSTERY DONOR**?

SORRY. EVERYTHING ABOUT THIS IS A MYSTERY.

IS THAT WHY YOU'RE **ALSO** DISGUISING YOURSELF?

CORRECT.

IN FACT, FROM NOW ON, YOU CAN CALL ME THE MINISTER OF HEALTH AND MYSTERY.

THE MINISTER OF HEALTH AND MYSTERY?

SOUNDS MYSTERIOUS, DOESN'T IT?

OUR GUESTS TONIGHT ARE HEALTH MINISTER **DR. ZUMA** AND THE **SECRET MYSTERY DONOR** WHO HAS PROMISED TO FUND "SARAFINA II."

TELL US, DR. ZUMA... WHY ARE YOU **ALSO** IN DISGUISE?

I CAN'T TELL YOU. IT'S A SECRET.

BUT WE ALREADY **KNOW** WHO YOU ARE!

BUT YOU **COULD** BE WRONG! ...WHICH MAKES THIS A **DOUBLE-SECRET MYSTERY!**

AND WE'LL BE RIGHT BACK WITH TONIGHT'S TOPIC-- "**TRANSPARENCY** IN GOVERNMENT"... AFTER THIS.

HI KID. RE-MEMBER ME?

OF COURSE I REMEMBER! YOU BROUGHT SARAFINA II TO OUR VILLAGE. I KNEW YOU'D COME BACK!

THINGS ARE A LITTLE HOT RIGHT NOW. I NEEDED TO GET BACK TO MY ROOTS. ...AND THIS PLACE HOLDS A LOT OF MEMORIES.

FOR ME TOO, SIR.

REMEMBER THE SINGING? REMEMBER THE DANCING? THE APPLAUSE? THE EXCITEMENT?

...REMEMBER THAT PETTY CASH BOX I ASKED YOU TO BURY?

YES, SIR. I MADE A MAP.

YOU THINK IT WAS EASY PUTTING TOGETHER SARAFINA II FOR FOURTEEN MILLION?!

AND TALK ABOUT UN-REASONABLE REQUESTS! THEY EXPECTED ME TO ACCOUNT FOR EVERYTHING! THEN THEY TELL ME I SHOULD HAVE CONSULTED MEDICAL EXPERTS!

THINGS GOT SO BAD, I EVEN HAD TO INSTALL A BRAND NEW RECORDING STUDIO IN MY OWN HOUSE!!

I TELL YOU, KID. I'M NEVER WORKING FOR THE GOVERNMENT AGAIN!!

I DON'T BLAME YOU, SIR.

TRUST ME, KID. EVERY PENNY I SPENT ON SARAFINA II, I SPENT FOR THE GOOD OF THE TAXPAYER.

TAKE THIS, FOR INSTANCE.

YOU... BOUGHT A BOAT, SIR?

YES... BUT I NAMED IT THE SARAFINA II!

...NOW EVERY SAILOR THAT SAILS BY GETS A FREE HEALTH MESSAGE.

MADAM & Eve

BY S.FRANCIS, H.DUGMORE & RICO

WHAT'S A CONDOM?

EVE!!

...WELL?

LISTEN... I'LL **PAY** YOU TEN BUCKS IF YOU GO ASK SOMEONE ELSE.

EVE... WHAT'S A CONDOM?

IT'S A "SARAFINA."

OH.

A **SARAFINA**?!! YOU CALL THEM "SARAFINAS" NOW?!!

OF COURSE! IN THE TOWNSHIPS WE HAVE **SLANG EXPRESSIONS** FOR EVERYTHING.

OKAY. I ASKED SOMEONE ELSE. WHERE'S MY MONEY?

WOW!! TEN BUCKS FOR DOING **ABSOLUTELY NOTHING!**

WHAT A **ZUMA**!!

MADAM & Eve

BY S. FRANCIS, H. DUGMORE & RICO

My first PRISON PHOTO ALBUM — GREG BLANK

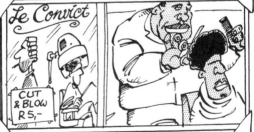

ME... WITH "BUBBA"-- MY FIRST CELLMATE!

ON MY FIRST DAY, HE ASKED IF I WANTED TO GET "MARRIED." I TOLD HIM "SURE...ONE DAY, IF I MEET THE RIGHT WOMAN!" WHAT A CARING INDIVIDUAL!

ME AND BUBBA SHARING A HEARTY PRISON BREAKFAST.

BELIEVE IT OR NOT, BUBBA AND I HAD A LOT IN COMMON-- WE BOTH MADE A KILLING IN THE MARKETS!... EXCEPT BUBBA ALSO MADE ONE IN A SHEBEEN AND IN SOME GUY'S DRIVEWAY. WHAT A WACKY GUY!!

ME... EXERCISING IN THE NEW PRISON GYM I DONATED! I RAISED THE MONEY ON MY CELLPHONE. GET IT? CELLPHONE!

(THAT'S A JOKE.)

MY GOOD FRIEND ABDUL B. COLLECTING MONEY FOR THE WEEKLY SOCCER BETTING POOL.

WE BET ON OVER 104 GAMES AND NOBODY WON!

WERE WE UNLUCKY OR WHAT?!

Le Convict — CUT & BLOW R 5,-

"LE CONVICT"-- OUR NEW PRISON HAIR SALON THAT I BUILT THROUGH HARD WORK AND GENEROUS DONATIONS. BUBBA BECAME QUITE THE HAIR STYLIST!!

ME... AND THE FREE M-NET SERVICE I ARRANGED FOR ALL THE PRISONERS.

IT WAS REALLY POPULAR UNTIL THEY SHOWED "ESCAPE FROM ALCATRAZ"!

AFTER THAT, ATTENDANCE MYSTERIOUSLY FELL OFF.

ME AND MY GOOD FRIENDS ON THE PAROLE BOARD. (LEFT TO RIGHT: BOB, VUSI, ME, KOOS & MARY)

THANKS TO MY ADVICE, THEIR NEW STOCK PORTFOLIOS ARE REALLY TAKING OFF!

SEE YOU ON THE OUT-SIDE, GUYS!!

© RICO 1996

WHERE AM I?

YOU'RE IN OUR SPACESHIP.

YOU MIELIE LADIES FROM OUTER SPACE... HAVE ABDUCTED ME?

YES. BUT DON'T BLAME US...

OUR PLANET SAYS WE HAVEN'T ABDUCTED ENOUGH WHITE PEOPLE LATELY.

YOU MEAN-- I'M AN AFFIRMATIVE ACTION ABDUCTION?!!

TOLD YOU SHE'D BE ANGRY.

MADAM! YOUR MOTHER'S JUST BEEN ABDUCTED BY MIELIE LADIES FROM OUTER SPACE!!

DID YOU HEAR ME?! I SAID YOUR MOTHER'S BEEN ABDUCTED BY ALIENS!!

DON'T WORRY...

THEY WON'T KEEP HER LONG.

NO GIN & TONIC?!! AND YOU CALL YOURSELVES AN ADVANCED CIVILISATION?!!

MRS ANDERSON...I WANTED TO SPEAK WITH YOU PRIVATELY BEFORE I TELL YOUR MOTHER.

YES DOCTOR?

I'M AFRAID SHE FAILED HER EYE EXAMINATION. SHE'LL BE NEEDING STRONG GLASSES.

THAT'S WHAT YOU THINK, YOU STUPID QUACK!!

ON THE PLUS SIDE HOWEVER, HER HEARING IS EXCELLENT.

QUACK! QUACK! QUACK! QUACK!

DID GRANDMA REALLY GET NEW GLASSES?

YES. SO WHATEVER YOU DO, DON'T MAKE A BIG DEAL ABOUT THEM.

HI. WHAT'S FOR BREAKFAST?

WOULD YOU EXCUSE US A SECOND?

HEE-HEE! HOO-HOO! CHUCKLE!

THAT OPTOMETRIST IS A DEAD MAN.

GO AHEAD-- MAKE FUN OF MY NEW GLASSES ALL YOU WANT!!

I DON'T CARE! AFTER ALL THESE YEARS, I CAN FINALLY SEE EVERYTHING!!

GASP EVE! WHY, YOU... YOU'RE...

...YOU'RE BLACK!

NICE TRY.

OKAY! YOU'VE ALL TRIED ON MY NEW GLASSES! **HAPPY NOW?!!**

LOOK COMMANDER-- THE FLYING SAUCER IS OPENING!

OH NO!! IT'S **HORRIBLE**! IT'S...IT'S...

...GIANT BUG-EYED MONSTERS FROM OUTER SPACE!!

WHAT'S ON TV?

AAAAH!!

THAT DOES IT. I'M GETTING CONTACT LENSES.

167

MADAM & Eve

PRESENTS:
SOUTH AFRICAN
SOUND EFFECTS

MADAM & Eve

BY S. FRANCIS, H. DUGMORE & RICO

HI! AND WELCOME TO THE **EVE SISULU SHOW!!**

THANK YOU. THANK YOU. PLEASE... YOU'RE TOO KIND.

CLAP! CLAP! CLAP! CLAP! CLAP! CLAP! CLAP! CLAP! CLAP!

OUR FIRST GUEST TONIGHT IS ABIGAIL ANDERSON. ABIGAIL -- WELCOME TO THE SHOW.

THANK YOU, EVE. IT'S GOOD TO BE HERE.

AND I SEE YOU'VE BROUGHT SOMEONE WITH YOU.

YES. THIS IS MY DAUGHTER GWEN.

HER DAUGHTER GWEN! GWEN -- WHERE'RE YOU FROM AND WHAT DO YOU DO?

EVE, I'M A MADAM FROM THE NORTHERN SUBURBS.

THE **NORTHERN SUBURBS!!** ANYONE ELSE HERE FROM THE NORTHERN SUBURBS?!

I AM!

GOOD. MAYBE YOU CAN GIVE HER A RIDE HOME!

HAHAHAHAHAHA!!

CLAP! CLAP! CLAP! CLAP! CLAP! CLAP!

DING! DONG!

AND THERE'S THE BELL! YOU KNOW WHAT **THAT** MEANS! -- IT'S OUR **SURPRISE MYSTERY GUEST!**

WHY,... IT'S **ERIC ANDERSON,** GWEN'S SON -- ALL THE **WAY FROM UNIVERSITY!!** ERIC -- WHAT'S THAT YOU'RE HOLDING?!

UH... IT'S MY DIRTY LAUNDRY.

...HIS **DIRTY LAUNDRY!!** GIVE HIM A **BIG HAND!!**

...IT'S AMAZING WHAT YOU'LL **WATCH** WHEN YOUR TV-SET IS **BROKEN.**

CLAP CLAP CLAP CLAP

CLAP CLAP CLAP CLAP

THIS IS SERGEANT VAN STADEN WE'VE JUST CORNERED ONE OF OUR MOST WANTED CRIMINALS.

YES SIR... IN ADDITION TO AN UNPAID PARKING TICKET... SHE HASN'T PAID HER TV-LICENCE.

LOOK OUT!! SHE'S GOING FOR THE REMOTE CONTROL!!

SIR... WE'VE GOT A HOSTAGE SITUATION.

NOBODY MOVE OR I TURN ON THE TV!!

WE'RE BACK! WITH MORE OF...

SOUTH AFRICA'S 100 MOST WANTED CRIMINALS

NUMBER 81 -- GWEN ANDERSON.

1906605010

ALSO KNOWN AS "MADAM."

WANTED FOR AN UNPAID PARKING TICKET...

1906605010

...AND NON-PAYMENT OF A TV-LICENCE.

MADAM! COME QUICKLY! YOU'RE ON THE TELEVISION!!

NEXT UP, EVE SISULU ...FROM SOUTH AFRICA.

GOING FOR HER GOLD MEDAL, EVE HAS SELECTED A TRIPLE REVERSE SOMERSAULT WITH A DOUBLE TWIST OFF THE HIGH BOARD.

THE CROWD GOES SILENT IN ANTICIPATION...

EVE!! ARE YOU STANDING ON THE IRONING BOARD AGAIN?!

...LAST MINUTE INSTRUCTIONS FROM HER COACH...

MADAM & Eve

BY S. FRANCIS, H. DUGMORE & RICO

CAN YOU IMAGINE IF DRINKING GIN WAS AN OLYMPIC EVENT?"

THEY COULD CALL IT... THE "GINCATHLON."

AND NEXT UP... IS MOTHER ANDERSON, REPRESENTING SOUTH AFRICA.

MOTHER ANDERSON WILL BE ATTEMPTING A TRIPLE GIN & TONIC WITH A HALF TWIST OF LEMON... A HIGH DEGREE OF DIFFICULTY.

THE CROWD IS HUSHED. AND-- YES! ...SHE'S REACHING FOR THE GLASS!

AND THERE SHE GOES! GOOD TILT... IMPRESSIVE SWALLOWING TECHNIQUE...

...AND A NEAR-PERFECT DISMOUNT!

BUT WAIT! OH NO! THE TWIST OF LEMON FELL INTO HER LAP! THE JUDGES WILL **HAVE** TO DEDUCT POINTS! WHAT A DISAPPOINTMENT!

YOU'RE TREADING ON THIN ICE.

NEXT UP, FIGURE SKATING.

MADAM & Eve

BY S. FRANCIS, H. DUGMORE & RICO

STOP! THIEF!!

WHUMP!!

HEY! COME BACK WITH MY TV-SET!!

PUFF PUFF PUFF · PUFF PUFF PUFF

ROWF! ROWF! ROWF! WOOF! ROWF!! WOOF! WOO WOOF!! WOOF!!

ROWF! ROWF! ROWF! ROWF!! R ROWF! ROWF!

ARMED RESPONSE! FREEZE!!

BLAM!! BLAM! BLAM! BLAM! BLAM!

I HATE WHEN THAT HAPPENS.

175